920
ZYM

WITHDRAWN

WITHDRAWN

GALAXY OF SUPERSTARS

Ben Affleck
Backstreet Boys
Brandy
Garth Brooks
Mariah Carey
Matt Damon
Cameron Diaz
Celine Dion
Leonardo DiCaprio
Tom Hanks
Hanson
Jennifer Love Hewitt

Lauryn Hill
Jennifer Lopez
Ricky Martin
Ewan McGregor
Mike Myers
'N Sync
LeAnn Rimes
Adam Sandler
Britney Spears
Spice Girls
Jonathan Taylor Thomas
Venus Williams

CHELSEA HOUSE PUBLISHERS

GALAXY OF SUPERSTARS

Backstreet Boys

Cathy Alter Zymet

CHELSEA HOUSE PUBLISHERS
Philadelphia

Dedication: *To my parents, for believing in me—and to Matt, for loving me.*

Frontis: *The Backstreet Boys' love of music drew them together, and their phenomenal talent has made them international megastars.*

Produced by
21st Century Publishing and Communications, Inc.
New York, New York
http://www.21cpc.com

CHELSEA HOUSE PUBLISHERS

Editor in Chief: Stephen Reginald
Managing Editor: James D. Gallagher
Production Manager: Pamela Loos
Art Director: Sara Davis
Director of Photography: Judy L. Hasday
Senior Production Editor: LeeAnne Gelletly
Publishing Coordinator/Project Editor: James McAvoy
Assistant Editor: Anne Hill
Cover Designer: Takeshi Takahashi

Front Cover Photo: Anthony Cutajar/London Features Int'l
Back Cover Photo: Anthony Cutajar/London Features Int'l

© 2000, 2001 by Chelsea House Publishers, a subsidiary of Haights Cross Communications. All rights reserved. Printed and bound in the United States of America.

The Chelsea House World Wide Web address is
http://www.chelseahouse.com

3 5 7 9 8 6 4 2

Library of Congress Cataloging-in-Publication Data

Zymet, Cathy Alter.
  Backstreet Boys / Cathy Alter Zymet.
    p. cm. – (Galaxy of superstars)
  Includes bibliographical references (p.), discography (p.), videography (p.), and index.
  Summary: Describes how the individual members of this group got together and the growth of their popularity in both Europe and the United States.
  ISBN 0-7910-5503-5 (hc). — ISBN 0-7910-5504-3 (pb).
  1. Backstreet Boys—Juvenile literature. 2. Singers—United States—Biography—Juvenile literature. [1. Backstreet Boys. 2. Singers.] I. Title. II. Series.
ML3930.B203Z96   1999
782.42166'092'2—dc21
[B]   99—37310
                                                                                                     CIP
                                                                                                      AC

Contents

Chapter 1
Sweet Sounds of Success   7

Chapter 2
Let's Hear It for the Boys   13

Chapter 3
Finding Their Groove   23

Chapter 4
All They Have to Give   31

Chapter 5
The Boys Are Back in Town   39

Chapter 6
Boy Wonders   47

Chapter 7
Millennium Fever   55

Chronology   61
Discography   62
Further Reading   63
Index   64

1

Sweet Sounds of Success

It was the kind of hot, sticky night in New York City that makes most people want to stay indoors. But on July 17, 1998, mobs of excited teenagers braved the heat and stood packed outside of Manhattan's famed Radio City Music Hall. The young crowd had reason to be ecstatic—they were just about to gain entry into the Backstreet Boys' first full-stage arena show.

The fans had been anticipating this moment for weeks. Tickets to see the Boys had been practically impossible to get long before the school year ended that June. In fact, when tickets went on sale, they sold out in just 12 minutes. But these lucky ticket owners were holding their precious entry passes tightly in their hands, waiting to hand them over to the person who would finally allow them to go into the famed Music Hall.

At last the gates opened and thousands of eager fans rushed in, happily pushing their way along into the hall, laughing and yelling. Some carried cardboard signs, some brought teddy bears or roses. The younger ones held onto a parent's or older sibling's hand. The space that was

---

Backstreet Boys perform in concert on July 17, 1998, at New York's Radio City Music Hall. Tickets for the show sold out in only 12 minutes.

empty and silent only moments before was now filled with an energetic, capacity crowd.

When everyone found their seats, the chanting began: "Backstreet Boys! Backstreet Boys!" At first the chant started quietly, but within minutes, it reached an ear-shattering, floor-stomping crescendo. The fans who weren't chanting sang their favorite Backstreet Boys songs. Others climbed onto their friends' shoulders to get a better look at the stage. At first, all they could see were roadies walking back and forth across the stage, checking equipment and moving things around. It felt as if they had been waiting forever for the show to start.

And it *did* seem as if it had taken forever for the Backstreet Boys to greet their New York fans. After years of being huge stars everywhere else in the world, the Boys were finally conquering America. Just nine months earlier, the Boys had sold out 3,000 seats at New York City's Hammerstein Ballroom. On the eve of their Radio City Music Hall performance, not only had they sold out that venue but their self-titled debut album was certified quadruple platinum! What's more, their third American single "Everybody (Backstreet's Back)" had shot to number six on the *Billboard* top-100 singles chart, and the video for the same song was a viewers' favorite on the MTV show *Total Request*.

The Backstreet Boys *were* back! Nobody knew this better than their fans. When the lights at Radio City Music Hall finally dimmed, the audience went wild. Between all of their screaming, chanting, and foot stomping, it was hard to tell when the show actually began. First, the spotlights that had previously been panning the crowd went black. Then the opening notes of "Everybody (Backstreet's Back)" began. At last an announcer's voice boomed over the loudspeakers. "Good evening, ladies and gentlemen. Welcome to Radio City Music Hall. We have a very special show for you tonight!"

Suddenly, two giant screens above the stage lit up with baby and childhood pictures of the Boys. "And now," shouted the announcer, "here are A.J. . . . Kevin . . . Brian . . . Howie D . . . and Nick! Ladies and gentlemen . . . THE BACKSTREET BOYS!"

When the five members of Backstreet Boys took the stage, screams of joy filled the hall. The sound was deafening. And there they were: Kevin, 25 years old; Howie, 24; Brian, 23; A.J., 20; and Nick, 18. Dressed in red, white, and blue nylon racing outfits, they moved around the stage, waving hello to their delirious fans and striking poses. The smiles on the Boys' faces matched the smiles of their audience. The group sang a snippet of the childhood song "If You're Happy and You Know It," and the crowd screamed back in response. When the Boys started trading off parts on a short introductory rap, the audience was on the verge of hysteria.

The band started jamming, and the Boys, with Nick singing lead, launched into "Let's Have a Party." It was the perfect song to kick off the show. And what a spectacular show! The stage was covered with 64 feet of reflecting industrial steel. The set's big movable triangles glided from front to back and side to side during each song. Amazing pyrotechnics appeared eight times in the course of the eventful evening.

Judging by the fans' reactions, they loved the show. The Boys were on stage for more

After touring Europe, Canada, Asia, and Australia, the Backstreet Boys were happy to be in front of American audiences. In concert after concert, the Boys continue to give their all to their millions of fans.

than an hour and a half, finishing with a reprise of "Everybody (Backstreet's Back)." Along the way Brian appeared solo, accompanying himself on guitar to sing "That's What She Said." For "Quit Playing Games (with My Heart)," Kevin played piano, Nick hit the drums, A.J. handled bass guitar, and Brian and Howie sang beautiful harmonies. By the time the show ended, New Yorkers had gotten their first real dose of Backstreet pride. And they were hungry for more.

After three years of believing in themselves, following their dreams all across Europe, Canada, Asia, and Australia, the Backstreet Boys were amazingly right back home where they had started. "This is our home country and we've been waiting so long to come home," said Howie at a press conference. "We took the backwards approach, going around the world and them coming back here." Added Nick, "We've always wanted to bring it back home. But we wanted to make sure we brought it back strong."

By now the story of how five handsome young men with beautiful voices came together in their love of music—and found international success along the way—is a well-documented part of Backstreet Boys lore. But it's also a tale filled with hard work and some major disappointments. In fact, it is a magical story of sorts, especially since the Boys first got their start not far from the Magic Kingdom itself.

It all began in 1993, in Orlando, Florida, the town best known for Disney World. Back then, no one even knew who the Backstreet Boys were because the group was still many months from being formed. The five future members of the group—A.J. McLean, Howie Dorough, Nick Carter, Kevin Richardson, and Brian Littrell—were then only connected to one another by their future fate (with the exceptions of Kevin and Brian, who are cousins). Though they each shared similar hopes and goals, they didn't yet know that soon they would all be members of what would become, in just a few years, one of the most successful music groups in the world.

Pretty soon Disney's Magic Kingdom would work its own brand of enchantment on the futures of the five boys, drawing them all together in one special place and changing their lives forever.

How did it all happen? Like all good tales, this one starts at the beginning with "Once upon a time . . ."

2

LET'S HEAR IT FOR THE BOYS

Even though Kevin and Brian are the only members of the Backstreet Boys who are related, everyone in the band is so close, they are just like one big family. In fact the Boys are so tight, it's hard to remember that they all come from different backgrounds, different circumstances, and different parts of the United States.

Kevin (a.k.a. Train)

Kevin may be the oldest member of the Backstreet Boys, but back home in Harrisburg, Kentucky, he grew up the youngest of three brothers. He was born on October 3, 1972, to Ann and Jerald Richardson. When Kevin came into the family, his oldest brother, Jerald Jr., was six, and Timothy was just three. The family lived on a farm, and the brothers spent their time riding dirt bikes and horses and playing in the woods.

When Kevin was eight, his family moved to a small town in Kentucky's Appalachian Mountains. There his father ran a summer camp. Kevin always had a lot of friends because every year, kids from all over the country

---

The Backstreet Boys are so close that they seem like a family. It's hard to imagine that they started out in different parts of the country, with a variety of backgrounds.

Kevin Richardson is the senior member of the Boys. He grew up in the mountains of Kentucky, where he began singing and performing at an early age.

came to spend summers at the camp.

Besides his family and friends, music also played an important role early on in Kevin's life. When he was old enough, Kevin joined the church youth choir. Sometimes he and his mother (who is Brian's father's sister) sang duets in church together.

But singing wasn't Kevin's only musical love. In his freshman year in high school, Kevin received an electric keyboard. Before long he was performing at restaurants, weddings, and school talent shows. These solo gigs turned out to be stepping stones to starring roles in local productions of musicals such as *Bye Bye Birdie* and *Barefoot in the Park*.

Soon Kentucky proved to be too small a place to contain Kevin's talent. Although it was hard for him to leave home, in 1990 Kevin moved to Orlando with the encouragement of his father. He had no problem landing a job as a tour guide at Walt Disney World. Eventually, he moved into other jobs, playing a Teenage Mutant Ninja Turtle and Aladdin in Disney's daily parades. At night he was a DJ at clubs in the area, always on the lookout for ways to promote his own music career.

Then, one day in the fall of 1990, something happened that would change Kevin's life forever. He was 19 when he was told that his father was diagnosed with colon cancer. Ten months later, on August 26, 1991, his father died at the age of 49.

This was the lowest point of Kevin's life. Being called the band's "serious one" may, in large part, be due to the impact of this event on him. Even though his father is gone, Kevin still tries to do things that would please him. He says: "As long as I do what makes me happy, without sacrificing my morals, and follow what I was brought up to believe, he'll be proud."

Howie Dorough was born in Florida. As teenagers, Howie, A.J., and Nick formed a trio and enjoyed singing in three-part harmony.

Howie (a.k.a. Howie D.)

Like Kevin, Howie D. was the youngest child in a large, close-knit family. Howard Dwayne Dorough was born on August 22, 1973, in Orlando, Florida. His three older sisters, Angela, Caroline, and Polly Anna, and his brother, Johnny, were all very affectionate with him.

And his parents, Hoke and Paula, encouraged all their kids to always work toward their dreams.

Howie and Polly Anna took their parents' advice. When Howie was in first grade, he and Polly Anna landed parts in a local theater's production of *The Wizard of Oz*. Howie played a Munchkin, and his sister starred as Glenda the Good Witch.

In 1989 Howie won a nonspeaking role in *Parenthood* with Steve Martin. He also appeared with Burt Reynolds in *Cop and a Half*. His resumé continued to grow and soon included several commercials for Disney World, as well as a role in Nickelodeon's *Welcome Freshmen*.

At this point, Howie could have easily traded in his amazing falsetto voice and his dancing shoes for the life of an actor. "Acting and singing are like one for me," he has said. "I was either going out for an acting audition or I was in a talent competition. I tried to keep them both equal so whichever one took off first was the one I was going to go with."

While he was making the rounds of the auditions circuit, Howie met A.J. It wasn't long before they both caught wind of another talented young performer—Nick Carter. The three started hanging out and passing the time together between auditions. They began singing songs in three-part harmony. Their voices sounded so good together that they decided to form a trio.

Brian (a.k.a. B-Rok)

Brian shared with Kevin both family ties and early experience in church choirs. Brian Thomas Littrell was born on February 20,

1975, in Lexington, Kentucky. His family loved music and was very active in their local church. Both his parents, Harold Jr., who worked for IBM, and Jackie, who volunteered at their local parish, sang every Sunday with the choir in church services.

Brian recalls that ever since he could walk, he was singing in his church choir. In fact he sang his first solo to 1,500 people when he was just six years old.

It was Brian's devotion to his family and his faith in God that helped him through an illness that almost ended in tragedy. Even though Brian was born with an undiagnosed murmur and hole in his heart, he was an energetic child who never had trouble keeping up with his older brother. But at five, he fell off his bike and got cut, which started an infection that spread through his blood. The family was unaware of it at the time. A few weeks later, Brian slipped and hit his head. After being rushed to the hospital, doctors told the shocked Littrells that Brian had a deadly infection.

He stayed in the hospital for more than two

Brian Littrell, like his cousin Kevin, grew up singing in church choirs in Kentucky. As a little boy, Brian battled a blood infection but amazed the doctors with a full recovery.

months. Brian's doctors firmly believed that he had no chance of surviving and told his parents to start making funeral arrangements for their young son. His distraught mother prayed for her son to get better. Pretty soon the infection started to clear up, and Brian became perfectly healthy again. Overjoyed, Brian and his family thanked God for what could only be a miracle. Said Brian, "I think that's why God gave me this gift to sing. So I can bless other people's lives."

After his full recovery, Brian sang in church even more often. He also performed in school musicals like *Grease*, and along with his older cousin, Kevin, he sang at family gatherings. They performed classics from barbershop quartets, '50s-style doo-wop, and contemporary hits.

It was Kevin who played a major role in bringing Brian to Orlando. And once he got down to Florida, Brian never looked back.

A.J. (a.k.a. Bone)

Whereas Kevin and Brian's travels led them to Orlando, A.J.'s life began in the Sunshine State. Alexander James McLean was born in West Palm Beach, Florida, on January 9, 1978. He is an only child. When he was four years old, his parents divorced. One night his father, Robert, left without a word, and A.J. never saw him again. This traumatic event was very painful for A.J. and his mother, Denise. Ultimately, however, it made them very close. Today Denise is the Backstreet Boys' personal publicity contact, and she handles all the press requests that the group receives on the road.

It was also Denise who recognized A.J.'s talent for singing and dancing when he was still quite young. She encouraged him to perform as much as he could. A.J.'s first acting job was as Dopey in a production of *Snow White and the Seven Dwarfs*. Even though he didn't have any lines, A.J. caught the acting bug.

When A.J. was 12, he and Denise moved to Orlando, and he enrolled in a performing arts school. A.J. took many singing and acting classes, but his favorite lessons were in dance. "Tap, jazz, ballet, hip-hop, gymnastics—you name it, I've done it," he jokes.

After school, A.J. made round after round of auditions. The payoff for all his hard work was landing roles in several television shows. One of his first successes was a part in the Nickelodeon series *Hi Honey, I'm Home*. To play the character of Skunk, A.J. had to shave his hair into a Mohawk and bleach it bright yellow. Maybe this explains A.J.'s ever-changing hairstyles today.

When he was 14, A.J. met Howie D. through his vocal coach. The two became very good friends and started to spend time and audition for different gigs together. Little did

A.J. McLean grew up in Florida. His mother, Denise, encouraged him to perform at a very young age. She now manages the Boys' publicity.

Nick Carter is the youngest of the Boys. As a toddler he would prance merrily around the dance floor in his grandmother's club.

they know how far their simple friendship would take them.

Nick (a.k.a Kaos)

Nick was a showman long before he met A.J. and Howie. Nick's parents, Bob and Jane Carter, claim that when their son was born on January 28, 1980, he entered the world with a passion for performing. At the time his parents were helping Nick's grandmother run a lounge called the Yankee Rebel in Jamestown, New York. It had a small dance floor, and according to Nick, "When I was real small, I used to get up there in my diapers and dance around."

When Nick was six, his family packed up their old Cadillac Eldorado and moved to Tampa, Florida. Nick and his sister, Bobbie Jean (B.J. for short), were best friends, and they spent hours wrestling and dueling with wooden sticks. Soon the family expanded with the birth of another sister, Leslie, and finally the twins, Angel and Aaron.

Nick loved living in his new home, and he blossomed under the hot Florida sun. He became even more outgoing. When his mother caught him standing on a tree stump entertaining an audience of flowers, she enrolled him in singing lessons right away.

Those lessons paid off immediately. In elementary school Nick won the role of Raoul in a local production of *The Phantom of the Opera*. Once he got his first taste of the stage, he was hungry for more. At just nine years old, little Nick started auditioning for commercials and local talent shows. After appearing in spots for the Florida lottery and the Money Store, he decided that he'd rather be a singer.

Jane took her son to audition to sing during the Tampa Bay Buccaneers' half-time show. To her surprise, Nick nailed the tryout, and for the next two seasons he was there every other Sunday, singing to thousands of football fans. As if that weren't enough, Nick also won first place in the *New Original Amateur Hour* in 1992.

Around the same time, Nick went to two auditions that would affect the rest of his life. The first was for *The Mickey Mouse Club*, a show that had been the launching pad for child performers since the 1950s. Some of the show's more recent successes include 'N Sync members Justin Timberlake and J.C. Chasez, as well as teen sensation Britney Spears.

The second audition was for a singing group, but not just any singing group. There to audition with Nick were his friends A.J. and Howie. The trio had recently added Kevin to the group because they liked the way his voice blended with theirs. They didn't know it at the time, but the group they were auditioning for would soon be known as the Backstreet Boys.

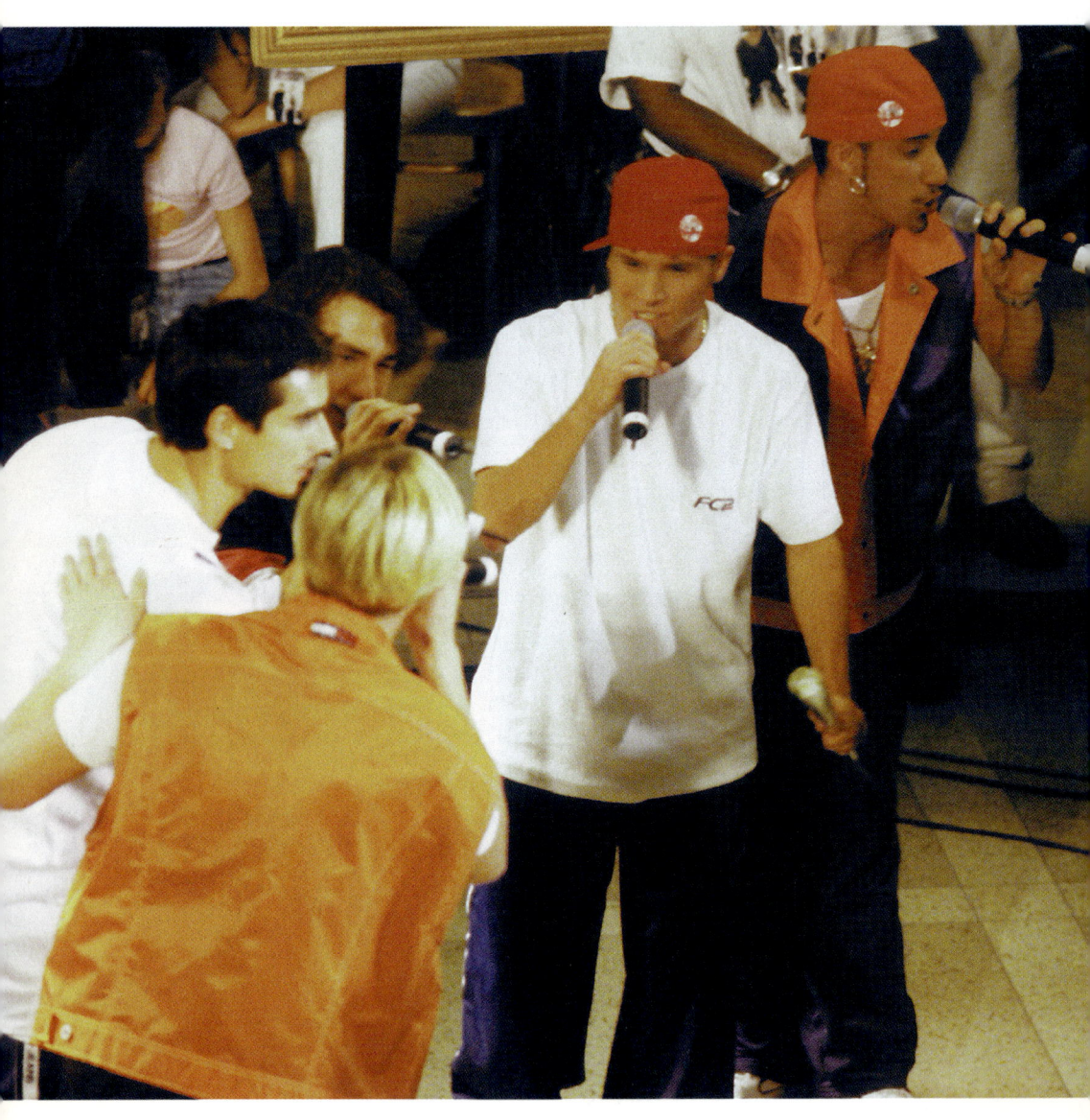

3

FINDING THEIR GROOVE

Lou Pearlman was holding auditions for performers interested in forming a "boy band." Originally, Pearlman had been involved in the transportation field, leasing jets to acts like Michael Jackson and Paul McCartney. That initial brush with show business made him eager for more. He became an entertainment investor, financially backing acts he believed would be successful.

Pearlman was hoping to start a record company and was looking for his first band to sign on the Trans Continental label. He hired some talent agents to place ads in local papers and set up auditions for 50 hopeful candidates. Four of them were none other than A.J., Howie, Nick, and Kevin.

The four aced the audition, but everyone thought they needed a fifth voice to round out their sound. Kevin immediately picked up the phone and called his cousin Brian. At the time Brian was in the middle of history class, but as soon as Kevin told him about the audition, Brian hopped on the next available plane to Florida. He arrived in Orlando the next day to try his luck at becoming the

---

The Backstreet Boys have worked hard for their success. Every number is carefully planned out, practiced, and perfected before it is performed before an audience.

group's fifth member. With Brian's voice added to the mix, the difference in their sound was beyond perfect—better than anything that Pearlman had expected. He signed them up with Trans Continental.

The band needed a name. The guys decided to name themselves after Orlando's famous Backstreet Market, a place where tourists and teens used to hang out and listen to music. In 1993 the Backstreet Boys were born.

By then the five had a name and a recording contract. The next thing they needed was someone to manage the group. Pearlman immediately thought of his friends Johnny and Donna Wright, owners of the Wright Stuff. In the pop-filled '80s, the Wright Stuff had guided the careers of both New Edition and New Kids on the Block. If anyone could help the Boys become big, it was the Wrights.

The Wrights liked what they saw—and heard. But they thought the group needed songs, moves, and fans. The best way to get all that, plus build a fan base at the same time, was to prepare shows and put them on at every high school and mall that would have them. The Boys even played over the loudspeaker at a pet store. The band recorded a single with Pearlman, "Tell Me That I'm Dreamin'," which they sold at shows. Within a year Backstreet Boys had become one of Florida's hottest groups.

Even though the Boys had cut a single, they wanted a record deal with a larger company. Donna knew just how to get them one. At a show in Ohio she called up her friend David McPherson at Jive Records. As soon as the Boys hit the stage, she held up her cellular phone so McPherson could hear them perform. What he also heard were hundreds of Backstreet fans doing what they do best—screaming. McPherson immediately signed them on.

Thinking it might have the next New Kids or Take That on its hands, Jive didn't want to waste any time. The record company flew the Boys to Cheiron Studios in Stockholm, Sweden. With the help of Denniz Pop, of Ace of Bass fame, the band produced their first single, "We've Got It Goin' On."

Jive released the single in early 1995, both in the United States and Europe. In America, where hard-edged grunge music was big, the silky-smooth "We've Got It Goin' On" only made it to number 69 on *Billboard* magazine's Hot 100 chart. But the single fared much better in England and Germany, where bands like Take That and East 17 were topping the charts. Explains Brian, "Over there they had a bunch of what's called 'boy groups,' so we had a ready-made market. But since we were Americans, we were a fresh new sound for Europe."

The single went into heavy rotation on English radio. By the time the group held an official launch party for the single at Planet Hollywood in London, it was obvious the Backstreet Boys had made an impression.

The Boys began making the first of several appearances on British television. They blew everyone away with their stellar performances on *Live and Kicking* and *Top of the Pops*. In the summer of 1995 the band hit the road, touring Europe with Duncan and P.J. Audiences all over the United Kingdom and Europe fell in love with the fresh-faced fellows from Florida.

REAGAN MIDDLE SCHOOL LIBRARY

The Boys entertain in concert during their first European tour. Audiences fell in love with the band's fresh new look, and the group was named Best New Tour Act of 1995.

On the heels of "We've Got It Goin' On," Jive released the band's second single, the ballad "I'll Never Break Your Heart." That number also climbed the charts to become the group's second hit. An early sign of Backstreet's success came at the *Smash Hits* Awards show in England, where the Backstreet Boys nabbed the prize for Best New Tour Act of 1995.

There was no stopping the Backstreet Boys.

"I'll Never Break Your Heart" went gold in Germany and reached number one in Austria. In 1996 they were voted Number One Boy Band by viewers of VIVA, a German music TV channel. By February the single and its video were in heavy rotation on both radio stations and music video channels in Montreal, Canada. The Backstreet Boys were now truly an international phenomenon.

And they hadn't even released an album yet. By 1996, fans in most of Europe and Canada were anxiously awaiting a full-length Backstreet Boys CD. At last, in April, the band released their debut international album, the self-titled *Backstreet Boys*. Along with it, the Boys released their third single, "Get Down (You're the One for Me)." Both the single and the CD quickly rose to the top of the charts.

But their fans demanded more. They wanted to see the Boys' many spectacular moves and hear their perfect harmonies *live*. Never ones to disappoint their fans, the Backstreet Boys set out on a European summer tour that included stops in England, Germany, Belgium, and Poland. This was the first headlining tour for the Boys, but they had nothing to worry about. They sold out every ticket for all 57 shows.

Their popularity showed no signs of slowing down. In September of '96, when their CD was released in Southeast Asia, it flew out of stores. In just 10 weeks, the album sold more than 600,000 copies. Their success in Asia prompted another tour, and the Boys made stops in Singapore, Malaysia, and the Philippines.

At the same time, the band was picking up more awards. In Germany they received the

Best Newcomers Award at the VIVA Comet Awards. Even better, the Boys beat out megagroups like Oasis and the Spice Girls and won the Select Award at the MTV Europe Awards in November 1996. Fittingly, Robbie Williams, who had just left supergroup Take That, presented the Boys with the award. It was as if he were passing the crown to the new kings.

To celebrate their MTV award and to end 1996 with a big bang, Backstreet toured Europe again, selling out shows in a matter of minutes. One such show at the Festhalle in Frankfurt, Germany, was broadcast live on Premiere TV. It was a chance for fans who couldn't get tickets to see the Boys' amazing live performance anyway.

As soon as the lights went down, the band exploded onto the stage, opening with "Let's Have a Party." They sang and danced and really got the crowd moving before they took it way down. Sitting on stools, they sang an a cappella version of "End of the Road" and "Just to Be Close to You" before building the energy again with "I'll Never Break Your Heart." Then Kevin went into the audience, shaking hands with fans during "Anywhere for You."

Next, a drum set rose out of the floor, and Nick came out and began to play a solo. Suddenly, Kevin was there to join him on piano. Showing off their instrumental and singing skills, they accompanied themselves on "10,000 Promises."

Repeatedly throughout the show, they humbly thanked their fans over and over in both English and German. It was a great Backstreet experience, the crowd showing their great appreciation for the band, and the band showing their gratitude by putting on a knockout show for the fans. A few months later, the live performance was released on home video. With *Backstreet Boys Live in Concert*, the whole world could sign on as Backstreet fans.

But the Boys also had one other treat in store for their fans. To end the year on a perfect note, they had recorded a special thank-you to their audiences for making 1996 so incredible. A single called "Christmas Time" was given to all members of the Backstreet Boys fan club.

By the end of the year the Backstreet Boys had done it all—hit records, sold-out shows, millions of new fans. What could they possibly do for an encore?

4

ALL THEY HAVE TO GIVE

At the start of 1997, Kevin, Brian, A.J., Howie, and Nick couldn't walk down a street in Frankfurt without being mobbed by admirers. While shopping in London, they used diversionary tactics right out of a James Bond movie to give the slip to the tenacious press. In Montreal the Boys had to escape through a tunnel under the Molson Arena to avoid the crush of fans waiting for them after their concert.

Back on their home turf in Orlando, however, the Boys could still appear in public and go virtually unnoticed. When they visited New York City, the only fans who acknowledged them were those who had traveled and seen them in Europe.

Although the Backstreet Boys were stars in other parts of the world, they still dreamed of having the same kind of recognition in America. Like kids who bring home all As on their report cards, the Boys wanted to show everyone just how far they had come. They wanted to make people proud of them—from their families and vocal and dance coaches to their neighbors and best

---

Although the Backstreet Boys were superstars abroad, their fan base built more slowly in America. But once audiences heard the group, they couldn't get enough. Here excited fans reach out to touch their idols.

friends from grade school.

The Backstreet Boys were preparing for a major assault on the American pop market and they wanted to give it their all. "It's a chance for us to show all of our friends and family what we've been doing for the past four or five years since we've been together," explained Kevin. "It's a personal thing for us."

During the early part of the year, everyone in the band eagerly went straight into the studio and spent many long hours recording their second European album, *Backstreet's Back*. They promoted the album heavily that spring, with tours and television appearances all across Europe and Canada. With all their globe-trotting, the guys still managed to fly back to Los Angeles in June, where they were going to shoot three more videos for their next three singles.

Shooting the videos was a very long and arduous process. Every video involved intricate choreography with split-second timing that had to be worked out in great detail, practiced, and perfected. After hours of rehearsing, the Boys spent more time in wardrobe and make-up. The results were worth it.

As Long As You Love Me and *All I Have To Give* were both directed by Nigel Dicks. In the former, the Boys used the state-of-the-art technique of "morphing." The video shows Howie morphing into Nick, who becomes A.J., who becomes Kevin, who changes into Brian. The video for the second song is more moody and has the band, dressed in shiny silver suits, dancing in and out of shadows.

Because the band had the original idea for the video *Everybody (Backstreet's Back)*, it became their favorite. They were on a plane ride when Kevin imagined that it would be very cool to do a 1990s version of Michael Jackson's *Thriller* video. The guys hired Joseph Kahn, a young director who had done videos for Shaquille O'Neal and was a pro at using special effects.

The video starts when the Boys' tour bus breaks down and they are forced to spend the night in a creepy old castle. Asleep, each guy dreams and then becomes a character out of a horror story. After each of the Boys acts out his monster role, the video culminates in a huge dance scene in the old castle's grand ballroom. The next morning when the guys wake up, they all compare what they can remember from their dreams, leave the castle, and then meet up with their bus driver—who's gone crazy!

Each member of the band got to pick the monster he most wanted to be. Howie took a bite at playing the mysterious Count Dracula. Brian thought he would make a perfect werewolf. Nick was wrapped up in being a mummy; A.J. starred as the Phantom of the Opera. And although Kevin showed both sides of his personality by playing Dr. Jekyll and Mr. Hyde, Nick thought he would have made a better Frankenstein monster.

All the scenes were shot in a huge airplane hangar, which was about the only place big enough for a castle. While the painters and carpenters got down to the business of constructing the elaborate sets, the Boys went right to work with their choreographer. They wanted to get everything perfect for the big dance-scene extravaganza.

The filming of the video was squeezed into just three days, even though the director originally thought it would take more than two weeks. That meant the Boys had to be up at 5:00 A.M. to do hair and makeup. Nick's makeup took the least amount of time, but still lasted four hours. Clocking in at six hours, Kevin's time in the chair was the longest.

Once the makeup was done, the guys had to be extra careful not to mess up their faces. They weren't even allowed to eat and had to drink through straws. Andre Csillas, a photographer on the set, remembers, "The one with the worst costume was probably Brian. With his false teeth, he couldn't even speak! Howie had quite the same problem with his Dracula's teeth. No, it wasn't lots of fun for them."

The Boys worked 14-hour days—days that felt even longer because of several glitches that occurred during filming. For example, Nick's part in the video required three straight hours of work, not including all the time it took to touch up his makeup. At the end of the day's shoot, when Kahn saw the film that was shot, there was a problem with the film, and the entire sequence had to be reshot.

Kevin's shoot didn't go any more smoothly. For one part he had to have live rats running over his head and shoulders. Kevin was okay with his new four-legged friends until they tried to crawl under his costume.

"I could see in Kevin's eyes what was happening in his head," recalls Csillas. "He was thinking, 'Either I burst out laughing and we have to start everything again, [or] I continue.' Well, he continued!"

Brian poses with an autographed copy of the Boys' second CD. In 1997 the group promoted the album all across Europe and Canada.

With their three new videos finished the Backstreet Boys were finally ready to reach for the brass ring in America. They launched their bid for fame by releasing the single "Quit Playing Games (with My Heart)," playing it for the whole world via a broadcast from Times Square in New York City. While the video began playing on MTV, the single debuted on *Billboard*'s Hot 100 Singles chart at number 24. Within two weeks it claimed the number two spot. The song would eventually sell more than a million copies.

Radio stations all around the United States supported the Boys. Both Top 40 and R&B-crossover stations were all giving airtime to the band's single. New York's Z100, a Top 40 radio station, and WPRO in Providence, Rhode Island, were among the first U.S. stations to add the Boys' single to their playlist.

"Quit Playing Games (with My Heart)" easily became one of the most memorable songs of the summer. To get their new American fans excited for the release of the *Backstreet Boys* CD, and to increase audience awareness about the group, Jive Records distributed a limited amount of official Backstreet Boys merchandise. Savvy shoppers could have scored with one of the 65,000 Backstreet Boys sampler cassettes that were packaged with the *Love Stories* series of teen romance books from Bantam Books. Subscribers to the *Sweet Valley High* book series also got cassette samplers. In August J.C. Penney also made samplers available with the purchase of Kaboodles makeup cases. The store also played Backstreet Boys videos on special screens in their junior department.

Stories and articles about the band started to appear in all the most popular teen magazines such as *16*, *Tiger Beat*, and *Teen Machine*, so fans could read all about their favorite new group. Some magazines also held contests in which winning fans could meet the Boys at their concerts or store appearances. Along with feature articles on the Boys, these magazines also included plenty of pictures of the attractive band members, as well as pull-out posters. Fans could have their favorite Boys hanging on their bedroom walls or greeting them from inside their lockers.

The media blitz seemed to work. American teens couldn't get enough of their favorite Boys. Backstreet mania had begun.

THE BOYS ARE BACK IN TOWN

By the time the full-length *Backstreet Boys* CD was released on August 12, 1997, American fans were waiting with open ears. The album included some of the same songs that had appeared on their two overseas releases, *Backstreet Boys* and *Backstreet's Back*, but the American effort really highlighted the evolution of the band's sound. Acting as spokesman for the group, Kevin commented, "The album has five of our singles that we released in Europe already—which were great songs—and we have some really great new songs added."

New tracks included a remake of "Set Adrift on Memory Bliss" (a song first recorded by P.M. Dawn); "If You Stay," which was originally on the *Booty Call* movie soundtrack; "Don't Leave Me," a catchy rock and roll sing-along; "Tell Me That I'm Dreamin'," the band's first independently released single; and "Tender Love," a song in which A.J. gets confidential, sharing the contents of a letter he has written.

That's not the only place on the record where they get personal. A.J., Howie, Nick, Brian, and Kevin share their

---

A wildly enthusiastic group of fans greets the Boys at the Virgin Megastore in New York City. The fabulous five were back in town to promote the American release of their Backstreet Boys *CD.*

hearts and souls in the album's liner notes. Dedicating the album to his father, Kevin writes, "He was the greatest man I'll ever know. If I can be half the man you were as a Father, a Husband, and as a Friend, then I will consider myself to be successful. I miss you Dad."

The liner notes also show the Boys' deep sense of religion. Each one thanks God before thanking anyone else. "First and foremost," writes Howie, "I'd like to start by thanking God, our Heavenly Father, for the gift of life and the talent he has given us to touch your hearts with our music."

This same strength of religious conviction extends from the Boys' album to their live shows. They have developed a group ritual before going on stage. "We all join hands and have a prayer," says Brian. "It's more or less a focusing point, with us saying, mentally, what we have to do. We pray for safety, that no one in the audience gets hurt or falls, because when you're dealing with a lot of people, sometimes it gets out of hand."

Things did get a little out of hand on the day of their CD release. Z100 hosted a major press conference for the Boys at the famous All-Star Café. The band was a little late because they were still in the middle of sound check next door at the Virgin Megastore. They were scheduled to perform there after the press conference.

When the band finally arrived at the All-Star Café, 300 reporters and photographers from all over the world had gathered. Journalists were eager to ask the Boys all sorts of interesting questions. One wanted to know if Brian really did sleep on a water bed. (He does. He bought a used water bed for $50 and sleeps

Reporters and photographers gather at a 1997 press conference at New York's All-Star Café. The reception the Boys received in New York gave them tremendous publicity for their upcoming European and U.S. tours.

on it when he's home.) Another reporter asked what it felt like to be finally getting recognition back home. Nick fielded that question, answering, "It feels soooo wonderful! It is truly what we have been dreaming about."

One journalist asked if the Backstreet Boys had a special message for their American fans. Howie responded, "We will be doing our best all the time! We hope to be an act that has something for everyone." Then the band showed off their new videos, including their favorite one, *Everybody (Backstreet's Back)*. After that, the president of Jive presented the guys with two special plaques: one honored their album for shipping gold; the other commemorated their new American gold single, "Quit Playing Games (with My Heart)."

After the press conference, Backstreet Boys headed next door to the Virgin Megastore, where a huge group of fans had gathered. The Boys serenaded the crowd with "Everybody," an a cappella version of "Just to Be Close," "As Long As You Love Me," and their solid-gold hit, "Quit Playing Games (with My Heart)."

The Megastore gig started a megastorm of promotional tours for the Boys. For the next few weeks they made appearances in Austria and Germany before heading back to the United States for what would be their first major home-turf concert. On September 21, 1997, Backstreet Boys played the Tupperware Auditorium, in Kissimmee, Florida, just a stone's throw from the Magic Kingdom. Like returning heroes, the band was kicking off their biggest U.S. tour right in their hometown, the place where it all started in 1993. In just four years, the Boys had gone from playing Orlando high schools to playing a major Florida arena. They were, without a doubt, stars.

Backstreet Boys' homecoming show was a huge success. They were a little slow to take the stage, and a lot of fans started screaming for them to come out. By the time the band appeared, posing seductively, the crowd was at a fever pitch. People stood on their chairs to get a better look, and the screaming got even louder. The band sang all their hit ballads, including "I'll Never Break Your Heart" and "All I Have to Give." They also showed off their latest dance moves, which caused even more screaming, especially for Nick. The show received a rave review from the *Orlando*

Backstreet Boys pose with their MTV Select Award in November 1997. The group had won the award for the second straight year.

Sentinel. With this glowing acknowledgment, the Boys left Florida at the top of their game and continued to take America by storm.

Next the Boys headed north to New York City. In the short time since they had last played there, their popularity had grown. Their September 30 appearance at the Motown Café was right out of the Beatles' movie *Hard Day's Night*. After the show, hundreds of screeching fans frantically chased the Boys all the way down 57th Street, one of the busiest streets in Manhattan.

That night, Backstreet performed in front of 3,000 fans at Manhattan's Hammerstein Ballroom. Brian admitted that he had stage jitters, even though he had done hundreds of shows before this one. "Before the show I was thinking, 'I'm not going to be nervous, it's just another show. I know it like the back of my hand,'" he confessed. "And then, right before the curtain dropped, I was thinking, 'This is New York City! This is America. Not only is this America, this is New York City!' I mean, how rough and tough can you get? How American can you get?"

By the fall of 1997, the Boys were not only stars of the stage but also stars on television. In October, November, and December, it was hard to turn on the TV and not catch a glimpse of America's newest sensations. The Boys showed up on *Today* and *Vibe*. On November 14 they sang on the *Ricki Lake Show* and hosted ABC's TGIF Friday-night lineup. Definitely one of their more laid-back gigs, the Boys relaxed on a sunny beach, joked around, sang bits of their songs, and introduced popular primetime shows like *Sabrina, the Teenage Witch* and *Boy Meets World*. On November 22 they boarded the *Soul Train*, a dance show that features performances by big-league artists.

In December the Boys were presenters on the *Billboard* Music Awards show, where they would return a year later not only to perform their music, but also to take home multiple honors. The Boys were also part of the all-star lineup for the Jingle Ball concert at Madison Square Garden in New York City, sponsored by Z100. The Wallflowers, another group that saw great success that year, and long-time rockers Aerosmith were also part of this yearly Christmas spectacular.

With all that these five young men accomplished in 1997—gaining American fame and worldwide success—it seemed as if they had already gotten everything they wanted for Christmas. There was one more present for the band, however. On Christmas Day the Backstreet Boys were the special guests on the 15th annual *Magical Walt Disney World Christmas*. This was a true gift, not only because they were back at the place where everything started but also because they were coming back as superstars. Performing from the Castle Stage, the Backstreet Boys felt like kings. And it was true. In 1997, everything they touched turned to gold.

Would the band still shine in 1998?

6

BOY WONDERS

Even though the Backstreet Boys had spent most of the previous year wooing American audiences, they never once forgot their loyal fans abroad. In early January, the Boys performed a live concert for Much Music, Canada's version of MTV, from the company's Toronto headquarters.

It was freezing outside and the concert wasn't going to start until early evening. Nevertheless, some Canadian fans gathered at 4:00 A.M. just to wait for the fab five to appear at the television studios. Despite the fact that the show had sold out in a matter of minutes, the fans still waited, hoping to catch glimpses of their favorite band. The police put up barricades to make sure everything was under control. By noon, however, so many people had lined up that the police closed off two blocks of one of the city's main thoroughfares. By 3:00 P.M. girls were being pulled out of the front rows because they were in danger of being crushed.

By the time the Boys appeared, the crowd was one of the largest the city had seen since the Beatles in the

---

Kevin (left), A.J., and Howie (right), show off their multiplatinum awards in Toronto, Canada. The Boys' live concert for Much Music, Canada's version of MTV, drew one of the largest crowds in Toronto's history.

1960s. Much Music had erected a giant video screen in the parking lot so the fans could watch the show being taped in the ground-floor studio. But the fans wanted the real thing, and they began pushing up against the television network's windows, yelling "Backstreet Boys!" and "We Want Backstreet!"

The situation was looking pretty scary, and there might have been a riot if the fans hadn't been so well behaved. Finally, the taping was finished, and Backstreet Boys made their escape. The crowd quieted down and made their way home.

After a bit more touring, playing gigs at Italy's San Remo music festival and appearing on French TV in Paris, the Backstreet Boys finally jetted back to Orlando for some long-overdue rest. Although globe-trotting throughout Europe may sound like fun, that kind of frequent flying can really take a toll. The Boys suffered from severe jet lag and constantly had to battle against disorientation caused by lack of sleep. Only Nick, who can fall asleep as soon as his head hits the pillow, seemed to have energy to spare.

Once back home, Backstreet had seven straight days off, which gave them plenty of time to get over the jet lag. But they had to make the most of their time off because it would be their last chance to rest before the next marathon world tour. For Brian, however, there were some major health matters to attend to before he could even consider heading back out on the road.

Unknown to the many adoring fans who had marveled over his recent stage performances, Brian was experiencing troubling heart problems. Brian's doctor told him that his heart had become fractionally larger, most probably because of his hectic and high-energy lifestyle. There was no doubt that at some point in the near future, Brian would have to undergo heart surgery. But until then he would have to be extremely careful about his health. That meant no more basketball—one of Brian's true loves. (That is how he got his nickname B-Rok.)

Brian was able to go ahead with the European tour. Once those dates were completed, however, he would need to have the operation and a full two months to recover. On March 8 Brian eased himself back into work and joined his bandmates for a few days' rehearsals. Once they perfected their set, they were off to a sunny, beach-side performance at MTV's Spring Break show in Jamaica. The guys wore matching combat pants and stylish hats and showed the reggae-loving locals how to rock Backstreet style. After the show the Boys flew to New York to sing on *Saturday Night Live.* The following morning they were in Orlando for a press conference before their evening flight to Ireland, the first date on their European tour. Already, the hectic pace was picking up.

Ireland, England, Denmark, Germany, Belgium . . . The Backstreet Boys needed their passports on an almost daily basis as they weaved their way through nine countries. The band was on an impossibly tight schedule, and they were beginning to show signs of stress. Nick, who hates flying, began to get edgy. Kevin complained of a strained voice and came down with a throat infection. And Brian, anxious about his upcoming operation, got more pensive than ever.

As the tour wore on, the guys became increasingly weary and began to take a hard look at the long-term goals of the band. Backstreet had learned a lot about the music business in the previous year. They began to understand that the reason they were being driven so hard so fast was because the typical life span of a boy band is only a couple of years. Backstreet's management was not expecting them to last much longer, and they were trying to get as much out of the Boys as they could. The Boys realized that in order for them to live on as a group, they would have to take more control of their careers.

Before they could think about their futures, however, Backstreet had to finish up with their present plans. They played their final date of the European tour on April 15 in Lisbon, Portugal, and then flew home.

While they were on the European tour, their popularity had moved up another notch in America. Their album had gone quadruple-platinum, and their single, "Everybody," had gone to number four on the charts. On Friday, May 8, Backstreet played at Disney's Magic Kingdom for Grad Night. It was an especially poignant show, because exactly five years earlier, the band had played a Grad Night show at Sea World. Five members appeared that night, but on this occasion, only four members were performing. Brian had to miss the show to go into the hospital for his operation. Before they took the stage, Kevin, A.J., Nick, and Howie all said a special prayer for Brian.

Brian must have felt everyone's support. His operation was a complete success. Hundreds of get-well cards poured in. As soon as he was healthy enough, the rest of the band went to

visit him. Reunited with his best friend and relieved that the surgery was over, Nick candidly admitted, "I couldn't picture life without him. Thank God everything turned out the way it did."

While Brian was recovering, the rest of the band worked on writing songs for their next album. They also took some time away from one another and caught up with their families and friends. Outside of the confines of the band, Kevin, Howie, A.J., and Nick had the chance to develop their own fresh musical sounds and ideas. This was a very inspiring time for the band. Away from their grueling

As busy as the Backstreet Boys were in 1998, they still made time to be a part of charity events. Here with singer Tony Bennett (third from left), the Boys perform for the "Storytellers" series which was created to help restore music education to America's public schools.

travel schedule, the guys were free to try many new things. Kevin even tried his hand at modeling, flying to Milan, Italy, to walk in a Versace fashion show.

On July 1, after two months off, the guys began intensive rehearsals for their first big all-arena American tour. Waiting to join them at the studio was Brian, fully recovered and raring to go. Backstreet had just six days to prepare for their coast-to-coast tour, which would include 30 dates in 24 states. Everyone was a little rusty after such a long time off, and they were eager to get their new routines up to speed. They worked with veteran choreographer Fatima Robinson on some inventive new moves, and before long they were ready to hit the road again.

Their summer tour began in Charlotte, North Carolina. Tickets to the 10,000-seat venue had sold out within hours of going on sale, further proof that their popularity in America had reached European proportions. The band unveiled a spectacular new show that also revealed some personal changes. Looking to exert their desire for independence, Nick tried out a new, slicked-back haircut. Brian grew some funky sideburns, and A.J. showed off some killer tattoos.

Even Nick's brother Aaron got in the act. Following in the footsteps of his big brother, Aaron launched his own singing career and appeared as the opening act for a bunch of Backstreet shows.

Everywhere the Backstreet Boys played, they were treated like real celebrities. From New York City to Kansas City, they were the summer sensation that everyone was talking about. By the time they played the MTV Video

Music Awards in September, it looked like Backstreet Boys were scaling to even higher heights of success. They also took home the Best Group Video Award.

But little did they know they were just about to go from the pinnacle of success to the depths of despair—both professionally and personally. In just a few short days, Backstreet's world would come crashing to a sudden halt.

The Boys perform before a full crowd in Charlotte, North Carolina, in July 1998. The concert marked the first stop on a 42-city tour through the United States and Canada.

7

MILLENNIUM FEVER

The joy of winning MTV's Best Group Video Award was quickly turned to sorrow with the news of a terrible tragedy: Howie's sister Caroline had died at age 37. She had been suffering from lupus, an auto-immune disorder, for a long time. Howie was devastated. He immediately flew home to Florida to be with his parents, his remaining two sisters, and his brother Johnny. The Backstreet Boys still had three more shows left in the tour, but they postponed their next appearance as a show of respect for Caroline and the Dorough family. Fans also sent flowers and sympathy cards to the family. Howie soon set up a memorial fund at the Florida hospital where Caroline had been receiving care.

In a message to the public, Howie wrote:

> The outpouring of emotion and sympathy I have received from the fans and the media has been overwhelming. Caroline was only 37 when she lost her battle with the disease called lupus. This disease affects the immune system, often striking young people like my sister in their prime.

Backstreet Boys entertain at the 1999 American Music Awards. The group overcame their personal tragedies and professional problems and moved forward toward the new millennium.

What made Caroline's death even more poignant was that it was preceded by the death of producer Denniz Pop—another person close to Backstreet's heart. On August 30, the man who help create Backstreet's signature sound died in Stockholm after a long battle with cancer. Like Caroline, he was young, only 35. Since Denniz had been with the band since the very beginning, producing hit after hit for the group, the Boys felt as if they were losing a member of their own family.

The Backstreet Boys also made a serious professional change. In September, the band fired their managers, Johnny and Donna Wright. It came as a big blow to the husband and wife team who had helped guide the band to the top. But the working relationship had become too strained. The Boys wanted more control over their future. Like the Spice Girls had done years before, the Backstreet Boys decided to manage themselves, with Lou Pearlman continuing as their business manager.

Believe it or not, there were more obstacles to overcome. The band was also embroiled in a bitter battle over their recording profits. Pearlman and the Boys sued Zomba, the parent company of Jive Records, for withholding royalties. Because so much money was at stake and the legal wranglings were going nowhere, the Boys decided to strike. They did not think it was fair that they had to continue giving 100 percent of their talent when they were not being paid a top rate.

If the Backstreet Boys refused to work, then there would be no more albums and no more tours. No one wanted that. It was a sad, depressing scenario, but the band stuck to their guns. Although the problems with the record company were not entirely resolved, an agreement was reached, and in November, the Backstreet Boys saw the light at the end of the tunnel. They flew to Sweden and began laying down tracks for their next album.

Backstreet finally had something to look forward to: As a show of renewed faith, they signed a deal on New Year's Eve with a new management company—The Firm. As 1999 began, the sadness of the previous year began to evaporate, and the Boys were filled with optimism.

The first few months of the new year went by in a blur of accolades. On January 6 the band was nominated for a Grammy in the Best New Artist category. A few days later, Backstreet performed at the American Music Awards along with such luminaries as Garth Brooks, Trisha Yearwood, Coolio, and the Dixie Chicks. Unfortunately the guys didn't take home the awards they were nominated for—Favorite Band and Favorite Artist. But that loss didn't affect them for too long. In February the Boys continued their winning ways when their debut album received the Recording Industry Association of America's (RIAA) Diamond Award. This means that their album had sold 10 million units.

Backstreet stayed on a winning streak, picking up Best Song at the Nickelodeon Kids' Choice Awards and Favorite Pop Group and Favorite CD at the 1999 Blockbuster Awards. They won even more honors at the World Music Awards, receiving an amazing four awards as the World's Best-Selling Pop, R&B, Dance, and American Group. It looked like they were taking over the world!

All this momentum was leading up to their

The Boys rehearse for Dick Clark's New Year's Rockin' Eve in New York City in 1998. The new year, 1999, brought the group even more accolades, including Best Song at the Nickelodeon Kids' Choice Awards, and Favorite Pop Group and Favorite CD at the 1999 Blockbuster Awards.

worldwide May 18 release of *Millennium*. A month before its release, Kevin hinted at what the album might sound like. "It's definitely the Backstreet Boys," he said in an MTV interview. "We haven't gone hard-core alternative rock or anything. It's the BSB sound, just more good music. Hopefully our fans are going to love it."

It had been three long years since they had recorded their last full-length album, and during that time, more teen-oriented talent had entered Backstreet's territory. Recent rivals included 98°, Britney Spears, and Backstreet's main competition—'N Sync. Were the Backstreet Boys worried that their new album would not measure up to the competition and their first album's selling record?

As usual the guys showed no fear. "We've had so much success on the first album, [it] set us apart from everyone else," said Brian, brimming over with confidence. "We're thankful we came first, but everybody that came behind us . . . we did a lot of opening doors [for them]. I think we'll continue to do that with this album."

One thing that made *Millennium* different from the band's other records was that this album featured the Boys' own music. Kevin wrote and even played piano on some songs, including "Back to Your Heart." Brian's contribution is "The Perfect Fan," a song that he wrote about his mother and which features backup by his high school choir. His mother, Jackie Littrell, cried the first time she heard it.

On May 15, to help get fans psyched for the album's release, Backstreet hosted their own show on MTV. All afternoon the guys played their favorite videos, including ones by Usher, Janet Jackson, Boyz II Men, and Coolio. They also revealed their goofy sides, joking about the time Nick got locked out of his hotel room wearing only green underwear and Brian's one-time job at Long John Silver's. The largest crowd ever gathered outside of MTV's studios for the program.

By the time Backstreet kicked off the release of their new album at New York's Studio 54, fans were experiencing *Millennium* fever. The album debuted at number one on *Billboard*'s Top 200 Album Chart, selling 500,000 copies in its first day of release. By the end of the first week, 1,134,000 copies had been sold, shattering the record previously set by Garth Brooks.

From the looks of things, Backstreet Boys will continue to break records as they continue to record and tour into the 21st century. But even as they garner more and more success, they never forget that it took years of dedication and hard work to get to the top. Remembers Nick, "That's how we got where we are today. We kept striving and working and never gave up."

Ranging in age from 19 to 27 in 1999, Backstreet Boys have accomplished things most people can never hope to do. They look forward to the future and dream of everything they still want to achieve. Howie would like to go into real estate and is beginning to develop condominiums on the east coast of Florida. One day Brian would like to have his own pop-gospel hour.

But no one in the band is ready to move on just yet. Says Brian, "We believe that as long as we focus on the music and don't get distracted by other things, we'll hopefully be around for a long time."

CHRONOLOGY

1972 Kevin Richardson born in Harrisburg, Kentucky, on October 3.

1973 Howard Dwayne Dorough born in Orlando, Florida, on August 22.

1975 Brian Thomas Littrell born in Lexington, Kentucky, on February 20.

1978 Alexander James McLean born in West Palm Beach, Florida, on January 9.

1980 Nicholas Gene Carter born in Jamestown, New York, on January 28; Brian almost dies of a heart illness.

1991 Kevin's father dies of cancer on August 26.

1993 Howie, A.J., and Nick meet and form trio in January; Kevin joins the group in March; Brian comes to Florida and joins the group in April; name the group Backstreet Boys.

1994 Sign with Jive Records.

1995 Release "We've Got It Goin' On," their first single; tour Europe; release second single; win Best New Tour Act of 1995 at British *Smash Hits* Awards.

1996 Release album *Backstreet Boys* in Europe, Canada, and Asia; film first video, *Get Down (You're the One for Me)*; receive MTV Select Award in Europe.

1997 Receive *Smash Hits* Award for Best Road Show; release "Quit Playing Games (with My Heart)" in U.S.; release U.S. version of *Backstreet Boys*; release *Backstreet's Back* everywhere but U.S.; first U.S. tour; *Backstreet Boys* and "Quit Playing Games" certified platinum in U.S.; receive MTV Select Award in Europe for second year.

1998 Begin first full-stage arena U.S. tour; tour in Europe; Brian has heart surgery; tour U.S. in summer; win MTV's Best Group Video Award; Howie's sister, Caroline, dies; fire management company, the Wright Stuff; file lawsuit against Zomba, parent company of Jive Records.

1999 Nominated for Favorite Band and Favorite Artist awards at American Music Awards; nominated for Best New Artist at the Grammys; receive RIAA Diamond Award; receive Best Song at Nickelodeon Kids' Choice Awards, Favorite Pop Group and Favorite CD at Blockbuster Awards, and World's Best-Selling Pop, R&B, Dance, and American Group at World Music Awards; release *Millennium* worldwide and 500,000 sell in first day; tour in summer.

Discography

Albums

1996   *Backstreet Boys* (European version)

1997   *Backstreet's Back* (European release only)
         Backstreet Boys (U.S. version)

1999   *Millennium*

Videos

1998   *Backstreet Boys All Access Video*
         The Backstreet Boys: Homecoming—Live in Orlando
         Backstreet Stories
         Night Out with the Backstreet Boys

1999   *Backstreet Boys*

About the Author

This is CATHY ALTER ZYMET's second book. Her features, profiles, and short essays have appeared in the *Washington Post*, *Spin*, *POV*, *Egg*, and the late, great *Might*. She lives in Washington, D.C., with her husband, Matt, and their parakeet, Mr. Pete.

PHOTO CREDITS:

Ilpo Musto/London Features Int'l: 2, 14, 15, 17, 19, 20, 30, 35; Sam Hain/London Features Int'l: 6; Craig Barritt/London Features Int'l: 10; Anthony Cutaiar/UCUT/London Features Int'l: 12; Kristin Callahan/London Features Int'l: 22, 38, 41; Awais/London Features Int'l: 26; Dusan Vranic/AP/Wide World Photos: 43; Rene Johnston/AP/Wide World Photos: 46; Kevin Mazur/AP/Wide World Photos: 51; Rick Havner/AP/Wide World Photos: 53; Ron Wolfson/London Features Int'l: 54; Ron Wolfson/The Shefrin Co./AP/Wide World Photos: 58.

Further Reading

Bronson, Fred. "Backstreet's 'Heart' Turns on the AC." *Billboard*, October 24, 1998.

Brooks, Amy, and Jeremy Helligar. "Where the Boys Are." *People*, September 14, 1998.

Dunn, Jancee. "The New Teen Spirit." *Rolling Stone*, May 27, 1999.

Golden, Anna Louise. *Backstreet Boys: They've Got It Goin' On!* New York: St. Martin's Press, 1998.

Jaeger, Lauren. "Everybody Packing in for Backstreet Boys." *Information Access Company*, July 20, 1998.

Johns, Michael-Anne. *Hangin' with the Backstreet Boys*. New York: Scholastic, 1998.

Jones, Steve. "The Backstreet Boys Hit Their Groove in Concert." *USA Today*, July 17, 1998.

Majewski, Loir. "The Boys Are Back." *Teen People*, June/July 1999.

McGibbon, Rob. *Backstreet Boys: On the Road*. Philadelphia: Bainbridge Books, 1999.

Nichols, Angie. *Backstreet Boys Confidential*. London: Virgin Publishing, 1998.

Rifkin, Sherri. *Givin' It Their All: The Backstreet Boys' Rise to the Top*. New York: Ballantine Publishing Group, 1998.

Rodriguez, K.S. *The Backstreet Boys*. New York: HarperCollins Publishers, 1997.

Websites

www.backstreetboys.com

www.ew.com

www.ashweb.com/bsb/

INDEX

"All I Have to Give," 42
All I Have To Give (video), 32
All-Star Café, 40-42
"Anywhere for You," 28
"As Long As You Love Me," 42
As Long As You Love Me (video), 32
Backstreet Boys
  and America, 7-10, 31-32, 35-37, 39-45, 50, 52-53, 55
  and Asia and Australia, 10, 27
  and awards, 26, 27-28, 53, 55, 57
  and Canada, 10, 27, 31, 32, 47-48
  and Europe, 10, 25-29, 31, 32, 42, 48, 49-50
  formation of, 11, 21, 23-24
  and future, 60
  and lawsuit, 56-57
  and origin of name, 24
  TV appearances of, 44
Backstreet Boys (album, European version), 27, 39
Backstreet Boys (album, U.S. version), 39-40, 41-42, 50, 57
Backstreet's Back (album), 32, 39
"Back to Your Heart," 59
Carter, Aaron, 52
Carter, Nick (Kaos), 9, 10, 11, 16, 20-21, 23, 28, 31, 32, 34, 39-40, 41, 48, 49, 50, 51, 52, 59, 60
Cheiron Studios, 25
Disney World, 11, 14-15, 16, 45, 50
"Don't Leave Me," 39
Dorough, Howie (Howie D.), 9, 10-11, 15-16, 19-20, 21, 23, 31, 32, 34, 39-40, 41, 50, 51, 60
"End of the Road," 28
"Everybody (Backstreet's Back)", 8, 9, 10, 42, 50
Everybody (Backstreet's Back) (video), 8, 32-33, 34, 41-42
Firm, The, 57
"Get Down (You're the One for Me)", 27
"If You Stay," 39
"I'll Never Break Your Heart," 26, 27, 28, 42
Jive Records, 24-25, 26, 36, 56-57
"Just to Be Close to You," 28, 42
Kahn, Joseph, 33, 34
Littrell, Brian (B-Rok), 10, 11, 13, 16-18, 23-24, 25, 31, 32, 34, 39-41, 43-44, 48-49, 50-51, 52, 59, 60
McLean, A.J. (Bone), 9, 10, 11, 16, 18-20, 21, 23, 31, 32, 39-40, 50, 51, 52
McLean, Denise, 18-19
McPherson, David, 24-25
Magical Walt Disney World Christmas, 45
Millennium (album), 58-59
Motown Café, 43
Pearlman, Lou, 23-24, 56
"Perfect Fan, The," 59
Pop, Denniz, 56
"Quit Playing Games (with My Heart)," 10, 35-36, 42
Quit Playing Games (with My Heart) (video), 35
Radio City Music Hall, 7-10
Richardson, Kevin (Train), 9, 10, 11, 13-15, 18, 21, 23, 28, 31, 32, 34, 39-40, 49, 50, 51, 52, 58, 59
Robinson, Fatima, 52
"Set Adrift on Memory Bliss," 39
"Tell Me That I'm Dreamin'," 24, 39
"Tender Love," 39
"10,000 Promises," 28
"That's What She Said," 10
Trans Continental, 23-24
Tupperware Auditorium, 42-43
Virgin Megastore, 42
"We've Got It Goin' On," 25, 26
Williams, Robbie, 28
With Backstreet Boys Live in Concert (video), 29
Wright, Johnny and Donna, 24, 56
Zomba, 56-57